THE EMPTY LOOM

THE EMPTY LOOM

Poems by Robert Gibb

THE UNIVERSITY OF ARKANSAS PRESS
FAYETTEVILLE
2012

ISBN-10: 1-55728-990-5
ISBN-13: 978-1-55728-990-2

16   15   14   13   12   5   4   3   2   1

Text design by Ellen Beeler

⊗ The paper used in this publication meets the minimum requirements of
the American National Standard for Permanence of Paper for Printed Library
Materials Z39.48-1984.

Library of Congress Cataloging-in-Publication Data

Gibb, Robert, 1946–
    The empty loom : poems / by Robert Gibb.
        p. cm.
    Includes bibliographical references.
    ISBN-13: 978-1-55728-990-2 (pbk. : alk. paper)
    ISBN-10: 1-55728-990-5 (pbk. : alk. paper)
    I. Title.
    PS3557.I139E67 2012
    811'.54–dc23
                                                            2012019375

Acknowledgments

Barnwood: "Days of Heaven," "Fragment," "Clearing Out the Closet"
Field: "Skunk Cabbage"
Florida Review: "There Were Flowers Also in Hell"
Fourth River: "Herbal"
Great River Review: "Morning Swim," "The Scarf," "Irish Catholic"
Green Mountains Review: "Elegy Roses"
Hampden-Sydney Poetry Review: "Orchards"
The Kenyon Review: "Mushrooms"
Missouri Review: "Monet at Giverny," "Florilegium of Wildflowers in
    New Homestead, Pennsylvania," "Blues Passage," "Garlic" (from
    "Garden Diptych")
Notre Dame Review: "The Empty Loom," "At the Hall of American
    Indians in the Carnegie Museum"
Poetry East: "Sonnet"
Prairie Schooner: "Mating," "Key to the Highway," "Li / The Clinging,
    Fire," "Braving the Elements"
The Southern Review: "Parenthetical," "Coming Again upon Mensch's
    Mill, by Accident, after the Passage of Years," "Birthstones,"
    "Groundhog" (from "Garden Diptych")
Sou'wester: "Edward Weston's Peppers," "Remission," "Drawing Her
    Bath"
The Widener Review: "The Configuration of Bodies in a Lunar
    Eclipse"
Willow Springs: "Looking at a Book of Paintings by Modigliani on a
    Rainy Afternoon" (as "Reclining Nude")

Parts I and II of "Before Summer Rain" appeared (in different
versions) in *Snail's Pace Review* and *Wind,* respectively, as "Figures
in a Landscape" and "Thyme: a Wreath."
    "Winter Storm Watch" appeared in *The Winter House* (Missouri,
1984).
    "Breaking the Soil," "On a Winter Night," "Mullein: Third
Trimester," "Journal of the First Birth," "Pokeweed, Persimmons"
(as "Pokeweed," and "Persimmons") appeared—some in markedly
different versions—in *Momentary Days* (Whitman Center, 1988).

"The Empty Loom" also appeared in *Notre Dame Review, The First Ten Years*, ed. by John Matthias and William O'Rourke (Indiana: University of Notre Dame Press, 2009).

Acknowledgement is also due to the Pennsylvania Council on the Arts, a grant from which was crucial in the completion of this manuscript.

Lastly, my debt to Enid Shomer, for the clarifying perspective which helped this book find its final shape.

Contents

I

II

BEFORE SUMMER RAIN

i.

We are in the garden beyond the barn,
A day moon fading above us,
The sun bearing down,

Its choirs in the hedgerows and nettles,
Its light in the ripening wheat.
Turning from the hoe,

I see that scalloping of bone
Along your spine—
Discs of pure candescence

Curved among the pole beans—
And watch myself watching
As in a dream I've wakened from

Once before: the bowl of landscape
Beneath a cloudless sky,
Cicadas at fever-pitch,

And then, as though spliced in time,
That scalloping of bone
Along your spine flashing as you rise,

Basket canted on your pelvis,
The recurrent afternoon
Now harvested as well.

ii.

"Fresh thyme," you sing, coming in
From the yard, cuttings
Carried in the lap of your skirt.

It is Sunday, midsummer,
And the small bracts fill the house
With a scent more savory and apt

Than any I've breathed in church.
A titmouse, the color of the porch trim,
Flits back and forth from its nest.

On the radio, Bach goes on plaiting
The gold strands of his music—
One of the *Brandenburg*'s, I think,

Clear notes in their cathedral of air,
Wreathing it like leaves.
Though evangelists crowd the channels

For the rest of the day, voices reedy
With Jesus, come bedtime, a few leaves
Still clinging to your skirt,

It is not our house will be troubled
By the calculus of song, your sweet oils
Wreathed in thyme's fragrance.

iii.

I switch off the light and watch
As the limbs of the chestnut take shape
Before my door, the wet leaves lit,

Again and again, by the dense tungsten
Strobes of the lightning.
If you were home right now,

I'd marvel at the way your body
Grows electric in such weather as this.
I'd follow the storm of ozone

Down into your dark. Alone instead,
I'll watch the fireflies glowing
Inside the shelter of the leaves,

Like a cluster of small yellow stars.
The densest of glimmers, except for you,
In whose body surge such storms.

MUSHROOMS

i.

After rain, after weather, they emerge,
Flesh-colored and naked as throats: milk caps
And parasols and slippery Jacks. They loll,
Slouch-brimmed or sprawling on their stalks,
Pale slips swelling upward almost visibly
Through duff and loam and pine straw.

ii.

Beneath the high leafed portico of the oaks
We found them rounded upon their nipples,
Fume-holes smoky with spores whenever
We tapped that fruit. *Gemmed puffballs,*
The book said, but these looked like untanned
Leather, bunched together above the roots.

iii.

Hunting them, we scrounged a fugitive
Musty crop—little pavilions of the body,
Horn and gill, the flesh sown broadcast in parts.
Theirs is the resurrection I can believe in,
Tonguing the faint tang of decay in the body
Of another, damp and tasting of the earth.

BREAKING THE SOIL

Stines Corner

Now in June—the wren ascending into the basswood,
The canes of the roses curving into bloom—

I lean upon the arm of the hoe, wanting nothing
But the opening of each outward arc.

The topsoil spreads before me in small, even curds:
A way of measuring my way these mornings

With their distances and bells, evenings
The light spills softly from its sources in the earth.

I don't want to be anywhere else except maybe
Sooner, and there only if it meant arriving

A little brighter and less bruised. Here, on the verge
Of time's couch and plenitude, I'd like to be

Through with arrivals. It's taken me nearly 40 years
To shuck my little handful of understandings.

I'd like to have some time now in which to move
Among them, sorting out the bells of morning

From the bells of evening light. I'd like to hull
The merely reflexive, first-person pronoun

And layer it upon the compost where it might do
Some good. Hoeing up another pocket of stones,

I think of my father's weekends hauling rocks
In order to wall the garden my stepmother thought

She'd like, of that patch I dug a few years back
For a woman the color of quartz.

Beyond me in the kitchen with its great fir beam,
My love goes about her rhythms, setting the table

With wooden bowls, lighting the stiff-wicked
Candles. I love how her black hair cascades,

Nights she arcs above me, flesh of our love together,
As though trellised with dark wild grapes.

PARENTHETICAL

The friend who introduced us still can't get over
Your great torrent of black hair
And wide regarding eyes, that dance-class air
Masking your reserve. For another

It's our pasture garden and the Angelus
Of light around you, backlit
At the end of an August day. "The pick of the litter,"
I called you once, teasing but serious.

Your slip shimmered on the bathroom door
Softly as the northern lights,
That first summer I followed your footprints—
Shining parentheses—across the floor.

HERBAL

The first time you saw it
You made fun of me
For laying my garden out in rows

As though stuck in ruts,
Then made your point directly,
Plotting a shape round as a pie-chart

In which your herbs would grow—
The backyard patch
I kidded was all off kilter,

Like a wheel with bentwood spokes,
All skewed, willy-nilly,
Into wedges of dirt.

But really I loved the way
It all went winding to where
You got in on the creation,

Tending seedlings you'd clip in turn
Or bring in by the roots,
Our house grown rich

With the scents of herbs,
Peg-strung bunches
Airing their oils until preserved.

POKEWEED, PERSIMMONS

i.

You want them for your weaving,
          The bright tang of their dye,
Want to slip your gloved hand down the clusters,
          Milking purple from the vibrant stems.

Color is a fruit you gather
          Along the edges of dirt roads,
The dusty acres of vanished corn.
          Strand after strand, you fill your jar with sunsets,

Crownfire, the mortal blaze in the weeds.
          A vireo flies above you—
Its eye bloodstone and berry and moving away,
          Smooth saucer to all that wine.

ii.

The cats are not persimmons and yet
          They share those qualities of placement
And form Mu-ch'i gave to his lidded fruit.
          Weston's peppers have it too,

That swirl of weight and presence,
          As if the flesh were any surface
Beauty gathered upon. Or in.
          The way, these mornings, light streams across

The two gray cats on our porch,
          And you, fresh from your shower,
Step into the full sheen of that image
     You find gleaming within the glass.

EDWARD WESTON'S PEPPERS

Even he admitted the dilemma.
How in *Pepper No. 14,* for example,
Instead of his abstract bundle
Of texture and tone and form

A viewer might see lovers
In a seated embrace, their bodies
Fused together amid the Rorschach
Clutter of their clothes.

For one, it's the petaled vulva,
For another, the injunction to savor
The folds of light which fall
On the perishable world.

All the same, he kept pursuing
The Absolute in each of its particulars,
As if it were there for the picking
And the photograph a koan

Of how things expressed an essence
Other than their own—
"Something more than pepper . . .
beyond the world we know."

While he cast about in theories
The photographs piled up, asking
What essence could ever rival
The nude, archival fruit.

LOOKING AT A BOOK OF PAINTINGS BY MODIGLIANI ON A RAINY AFTERNOON

Reclining Nude, c. 1919

Body like taut fruit, that could be you
    On the couch, undulant and flushed
        With sleep, flesh the color

Of nectar glazed in skins across
    The soft green undertones. Even at rest
        She's been made to flow

From the flattened breasts on down
    To the warm lap turned towards us—
        As if there could be no luxury

Like this, or sun in which to unfold.
    Back in her nakedness and clothes
        The model's been gone for hours,

But the painter who framed her
    In that drowse of light falling into
        His rooms, what's become of him?

Having checked her watch and knocked
    Again on the locked studio door,
        And having, as she noted, nothing

Better to do, Anna Akhmatova
    Has begun to toss the red roses
        She'd brought him, one by one,

Up through the open transom—
    A gesture she'll think to trace for us
        In her memoir's tender prose.

And Modigliani, inexplicably gone
    With his thirst and tuberculosis
        Into the welter of Parisian streets?

Returning, he'll find himself astonished
    At both the sexual fact of the flowers
        And the way they seemed composed,

He later told her, as though
    They had fallen from the painting
        Like petals in a ravished spray.

DAYS OF HEAVEN

When you were still a shy bride I could make you blush,
Reciting from that song of Ishtar's: "Plow my vulva."

*

Stines Corner was farms and shagbark hickories, herons,
Our small house lit by the constellations

*

And Coleman Hawkins' "Sweet Lorraine," circa 1943.
Teddy Wilson and Lady Day. Early Count Basie.

*

Evenings, barnstorming swallows would fill the skies
With the skittering, quick pivots of their flights.

*

The black shapes of Angus blotted light in their field.
Deer filed through the pleached aisles of the orchard.

*

We watched bluegills flashing in a lily pond, the nests
They cratered, stirring up clouds of silt from the bed.

*

The morning you came back to bed and straddled me
Your skirt floated about us like those lilies.

MONET AT GIVERNY

When the rain stopped giving pavements
Their surfaces of oil, the day grew luminous

With poplars and the gardens where we walked
In Giverny in the Metropolitan Museum of Art.

Painting by painting, we watched light change
With the time of year or day, watched as colors

From a warmer world took shape all around us.
I could see something of those trees in the line

Of your spine as you stood staring into sunsets
Which were haystacks and fields, the ponds

In which clouds bloomed like lilies, their petals
Alizarin crimson. And thought I saw something

Of Monet himself in straw hat and beard,
His fingers wrinkled as tubes of paint, there

Where the banked fires of flowers floated upon
Their gessoes. In the end, water bore him

More lightly than ever among cataracts, age,
The deaths of his friends—an old man tending

Surface reflections, the worn paths and bridges
Where he passes into his life, his work,

The children he's buried, the freighted canvases
He won't survive. For years now the full moons

Rising through the poplars have cast their light
Across that Giverny framed above our bed:

Silhouettes the winds play, leaves like shoals
Of fish, their black flames shimmering in waves.

Unmoored, we lie down nightly upon the waters.
Mornings we're borne naked back to shore.

LUNAR

Some nights you rise
                    on all fours on the bed
And look, wondering *Is it now?*
Has it started? Wondering,
                    you once told me,
Whose body this is,
Which is capable of such sacraments.

I'd thought that none of the mysteries
Could flow any deeper
Than your own blood's neap and tow,
The ritual of those waters sluicing through you,
Alluvial,
            phased to the frames of the moon.

A wound like a welling within petals
And you the bed of its bloom.

THE CONFIGURATION OF BODIES IN A LUNAR ECLIPSE

From our bedroom window,
Tucked beneath the tent of the eaves,

We watched the wafer of the full moon
As it vanished among the trees—

A shadow thrown out upon the sky,
You remembered, as though space

Were fabric after all, whole cloth
The stars burned through.

Lying on your belly beside me,
Your buttocks curved down toward

Your own dark cloud and crescent
Of night-filled flesh, your thighs

Were bathed with moonlight,
And the slant blades of your back.

Above us, that pale stone grew more
And more slender, the trilled pulses

Of tree frogs rising into the night.
When you slid into place upon me,

I could feel the distances tighten
And their longing to become spheres

Falling In line, the body of darkness
Curving across the body of the light:

One longing, and then another,
Centered upon its moon.

COMING AGAIN UPON MENSCH'S MILL, BY ACCIDENT, AFTER A PASSAGE OF YEARS

As though anyone's life looped back
    Through its own strange light,
        I am here again at evening, summer,

Watching nighthawks dart
    Beneath the scattered stars. Years ago
        We gathered here for the wedding

Of a friend's daughter, cars packed
    With beer we'd drain off, just up this hill,
        Backs turned to the in-laws.

Then we'd descend toward buildings
    Warm and glowing as hives, in love
        With how our shadows streamed

Like lines of darkness from the trees.
    Later, there was bluegrass and dancing
        And a kind of resigned forgiveness

For all we do too early or late, or timed
    To a private music hopelessly out of tune.
        Then we were there alone—

Four couples lounging on the lawn,
    The fireflies burning like fragments
        Of a world too dense for any dark.

Shadows gathered around us,
    The moon floating out upon the waters
        Of the pool, fenced to prevent our use.

That was the only time we saw
    The breasts of the wives of our friends
        Shining damply, the dusk of their sex.

All over again we learned the difference
    Between skin and flesh and the richness
        The body takes in women moving upon

The waters like oil. Now, years later,
    The fence we climbed is still locked,
        The diving board still stops in mid-air.

I think how well our lives fit together
    Back before the transfers and divorces,
        First stars appearing in their old slow fires

As we slipped off our clothes—
    That one, last, time—
        To swim in the lights we were born with.

KEY TO THE HIGHWAY

That evening we spent at the Maple Grove
Applauding a neighbor's bluegrass band
("Rocky Top" and "Rosie's Gone Again")
Through all three sets, you still didn't know

How to drive a stick shift. So when we got
To the parking lot and my bottle-green Beetle
You were surprised when I threw you the key,
Saying you'd nothing to worry about.

Buzzing with music and beer, I felt primed,
And we had nothing but back-country roads
("Little Maggie" and "The Lights of Home")
And besides you'd have it down in no time.

Which you did, cautious at first, grinding
Your share of gears, and me with my head
In your lap, shouting out encouragement—
Barely underway and transported already.

ON A WINTER NIGHT

Here it's not even seven o'clock
And already we've finished off the rest
Of that bottle of fox-grape wine,

Stemmed glasses flush with the color
Of wild sweet William in bloom.
If there were any more I'd pour it

And drink to the moles we watched
Tumbling in the snow. I'd toast
To the porcupine's tiny black hands,

The way it advances, upright
And bristly upon its mate—a thresh
Of wind through the spikeweed.

We'd have all evening to give
To the continuous inflecting of grapes
Into praise of mating owls

And foxes, a friend's new baby girl.
Sitting in the kitchen we'd wonder
If this year, for once, February

Might not shimmer with the last
Of winter's ice-wracked boughs.
That cassette we were playing

Would have reached Sarah Vaughn
Singing from 1945, "Lover Man,"
Her blue notes gracing the air.

WINTER STORM WATCH

We'd waited all evening for the sky
To come undone or not, your raffia

Hanging like a great braid of wheat
On the door, your pine needles

On the table, threaded from their tangle
In a bag. I'd barely sat down

To watch you plying pattern
Than the radio filled with Lester Young,

His limpid airy riffs. That evening
More than ever he seemed to me

Like light playing among the ice-
Enfolded branches of the trees.

North of us snow kept building
Those huge and ghostly auroras.

Darkness deepened. Everything seemed
To be gathering more fully into time.

I watched you there across from me
Testing the snap of your strands,

And thought if we could see beyond
Our windows—up to where the stars

Were bodies of primal light
Quavering above the airwaves—

We'd find nothing that wasn't here
Already in the quiet weave of motions

Filling our rooms. The evening
Would simply be Sunday, no matter

What storms came massing toward
That pause in the way things are.

MATING

You saw the male hawk first, soaring
From the woods along the ridgeline.
Saw his heft, the width of his wings,
The thick tail spread and banded.

A sight between the eyes—
You stopped the car so we might sit
In silence, watching while something
Perfect dropped from the air,

Then came together in the limbs
Of an oak with another, second
Of his kind. No dove ever descended
More sweetly. No tree drove its roots

More deeply into the earth.
All of it was theirs, a whole world
Engendering between them.
Lord, but he was lovely, watching

As she curved her beak into her prey,
Filled with herself, her roundness,
With the way he sat above her
Who loved her like the sky.

BIRTHSTONES

i.

It was like uncovering the foundations of the world
And digging them up, one stone at a time making way
For the great stalks of summer: sunflowers and corn.
Like lifting bricks from a buried kiln, chips of plate,
Ballast from the hold of a ship, astonished by how far
The scattered cairn sank beneath shovel and crowbar.

ii.

Those days when you were pregnant and hungry
For the distant sun, you lazed in whatever light
You'd found would bathe the warm fleshly sculpture
Of your shoulders and breasts, canted pelvis, the great
Belly rounding like a boulder on the fertile earth—
One stone at a time, like *touch-* and *blood-* and *birth-*.

MULLEIN: THIRD TRIMESTER

From over here I can't make out the pages
Which are filling your lap with names

For flowers and their intricate parts
Like a lapful of flowers themselves.

I can see only the tendrils hanging loosely
Along your neck, your face delicate

And tinged with shadows as the book
Into which you're looking, seeking

In each fluted blossom to find the name—
Swamp candle or *loosestrife*—

For the feeling that's been troubling you.
Perhaps it's simply autumn,

The arbors of light growing grainy
And harsh along the roads where you walk,

Or the sense that ripeness is only
A momentary swag of evanescence,

A weight inside you like water,
That sets you there, leafing patiently

Among the field guide's families of flowers,
Hunting for those tiered yellow spires

And the name which is wick to such
Understanding, laid out and clear.

JOURNAL OF THE FIRST BIRTH

i.

She dreams that we are playing catch
With human skulls
And that one of them is an infant's.

ii.

The body is a fruit which blossoms,
The flesh its swelling skin.

iii.

Are there better ways of marking passing time
Than by the steady ripening of this woman
I get to wake beside? Every day her calves
Grow denser, her breasts turn more to gold.

I watch as the soles of her feet press down
To span their fraction of the earth
And the one wing from her ovaries curves
Softly into bone, white as the flowering calla.

iv.
        8/1/85

Driving in this morning to the midwife's for Maggie's
monthly check-up—blood-pressure and weight check,
urine analysis—I thought of how division of cells
would soon be division of bodies, how union is only

preamble to dissolution and how we become human,
really, at birth. Which made it even more remarkable,
that heartbeat of a frightened sparrow. 140 times
per minute a sound like shook metal, or thunder from
storm clouds massing over water. Those "flashings-
forth" Melville wrote of, "those short, quick probings
at the very axis of reality."

v.

For blood is body to the light.

vi.

And now the downy whorl of hair,
Teeth like kernels
At the small end of the cob

And now that flowering stalk,
The spine, curves
In its fluted translucence

And the brain begins to densen
Like a lodestone
Sending out its net of red waves

vii.

Little dreamer, I think of you
Slumbering among counselors
And kings, the mother mass
Around you like the inner walls
Of creation, which they are:

Omphalos from where everything
Streams outward into its life,
As you will do soon enough.
But, for now, the watery cradle
Of the pelvis is world enough

And more than you can know.
You'll have time to learn things
Move apart, that the heavens
Are hollowing outwards
Like a tossed handful of stones.

That the turtle goes lumbering
In its shell, the lobster across
The Kansas of the sea-floor.
You'll have time, I hope, to heal.
Son or daughter, this world

You never asked to enter
Is Eden enough to break the heart
With longing and remembrance,
To fist the heart with hatred
At viciousness and greed.

Being born for the first time
Is no easier, no more lasting
Than the births to come.
It is my own life's course I follow
Calving into your blood.

viii.

It's been a blue week, child:
Rainy, November,

Mists on the ridges,
The sounds of gunfire in the woods.

Yesterday, after your mother
Labored all night to open
Into the corridors of earthlight
And starlight, they sliced you out.

She was cold, lonely,
And afraid for dark waters, the fish
That glide their hungers
Along the bottom of the sea.

I stood watching the while
They hauled you up, blue
As bottom clay, your tiny head
Alone there at the heart

Of the immensities,
And then your body
In a sudden gush flopped sliding
Among the entrails.

They knotted your navel
Like a small blue rose,
Then inked the pads of your feet.
This morning, keeping to the roads,

I felt more than ever
How the body is the first splendor,
And the mists, this November,
Cling to it like the light.

ix.

I take you up
And lay you down for the first time
Upon the earth,
My bright cub, quickness,
Ark-ribbed son.

for Matthew

FRAGMENT

The great dates of history, said Borges,
Go unrecorded,
              but here this morning
We wake to find that last tie to the fullness,
The dried umbilical knot,
                    fallen off
In the bassinet.

12/21/85

SKUNK CABBAGE

for Andrew

Finally, today, I found some
In the boggy margins of the creek,

Green caps belling upwards
Into the spring profusions,

The sopping ground around them
Littered with last year's debris.

When your water broke, that second
Time, flooding the bedroom floor,

You were already into labor,
Pelvis fissuring, the deep cleft

Of your body unfurling its clamped
Rhythmic spasms. There too

I could feel the planet gathering
Beneath my feet, the way

The deaf feel music in their bones.
Such flexed, slow florescence!

All through the delivery
You gasped and splayed, opening

For that blood-covered bulb.
This February I looked for them

Melting their slender chimneys
Where the sun's granular dazzle

Lit the remaining banks of snow.
I dreamt of them as storm clouds

Massing warm spring rains our way.
And of that lotus of a body

Lifted above its waters, umbilical
Flashing like a long, wild root.

MORNING SWIM

A sleek seal in your black, one-piece suit,
You swam laps those mornings before work
In a pool full of old men, charmed
By the fact of your pregnancy.

Each day they watched the water
Take more of your weight before parting for it.
They marked your progress,
Making sure they stayed out of the way.

You held them all in sway. Held me
As well as that body on the ultrasound screen,
Dancing in its flask of static.

Right to the end you made quite the splash—
Plunged, confluent, changed by the months,
A selkie in your element.

THE EMPTY LOOM

i.

Hiking through the Lake District, you watched sheep
Graze among the evening hills like a dusky, curd-
Shaped cumulus. Looms weave such clouds as these.

ii.

In his *Il Libro dell' Arte,* Cennini wrote that women
Took up spinning after squandered Paradise,
But surely he was also thinking of the roundness
To their rhythms in the soft Italian nights, the moon,
Pale bobbin, coming on . . .

iii.

I'm sure he would have loved the simple buoyancy
Of these heddles, the warping board, and the way
The wood looks like it could burn even under water.

Have loved the sight of you in evening light, seated
By the window, inching your patient fabric past the edge
Of the fell where the patterns gathered into cloth.

AT THE HALL OF AMERICIAN INDIANS
IN THE CARNEGIE MUSEUM

1. Ghost Dance Shirt

Pressed surplice, the color of the cover of a drum,
Of the Drying Grass Moon, fringed and cryptic,
Millenarian, Sioux.
               They wore them believing,
The feathers, the rainbows flashing at their sleeves,
Red stars spangling the yokes. Shirts like this one
Patterned from a dream: talismans against the guns
Of the Bluecoats, they were told.
                       At Wounded Knee
The stiff, shirted bodies lay dead in the snow.

2. Sky Chart

A room like an earth lodge, round and domed.

In here, where the hooped heavens slowly wheel,
The Dark God flings his stars upon the ceiling—
Time, seasons, passages on the earth all charted,

Down to the last crystal in the southern sky.
During the first rounds of radiation you loved
To sit here, quietly healing into the constellations.

The last one you saw they called Awaits the Dawn.

3. Rattle

Because, as you'd read, *the rhythms come from it,*
The Star Company's rattle is circled like the sun,
All the elements of the vast world fashioned there.
I can still hear you listing them for our young sons:

Wood, pebbles, paint, Sage Grouse tail feathers,
Great Horned Owl body and wing feathers—
Tracing each back to the rattle—*rawhide, tanned hide,*
Sinew, dye . . . as if the list might go on forever.

4. Baskets

From the roots of Western red cedar and Sitka spruce,
From the cinched, rolled coils of the yucca,
Handled or lidded, platter or canister or bin,
And gradient, woven to weights and measures . . .

You made yours from pine needles and raffia,
Patterned with dyes you strained from pokeberries,
The obsidian waters in which walnuts had soaked,
And from the blood where you'd stabbed your thumb.

When they were young, you told our sons that death
Meant changing into something light-filled, like a tree,
The blown wings swirling from it, or a raft
Like a basket, cinched tautly to carry us across.

THE SCARF

And I said, let grief be a fallen leaf
—Patrick Kavanagh, "On Raglan Road"

Grief in the ashes, grief in the basket
Filled with the last of your clothes.

And in the scarf, hand-loomed and woolen,
With its colors from the dark end

Of the spectrum—muted bands of coral
And madder and plum, finished off

With knotted tassels. You're posed with it
In the snapshots I'm looking at, the ones

With all the flowers from your birthday:
A dozen eruptions of hot-house blossom

And you kneeling in their midst,
Surrounded with colors as rich as Monet's.

Grief's there in the tumor
But we don't know it. Months will pass

Before your right arm starts to throb.
In the photos it's the near one the scarf

Enfolds, shawled across your shoulders.
I teased a smile from you at the end,

Wearing it flung around my neck.
Look what I found lying in the closet!

I wore it for your scent, your soft palpable
Presence, burying my face in its folds.

LI / THE CLINGING, FIRE

This hexagram, divided within and without,
is an image of the meshes of a net in which
animals remain snared.
        —The Book of Changes

i.

A tom in full regalia, tail fanned wide,
Drum-stick head at an angle, imperious and high.
I watch him strut around my parked black car,
Affronted by what he's found there
Mirrored in the clear-coat—
Beard and wattles, the wampum-beaded throat.

On display, he's been trying to drive the other
Away from its covert in the fender
And now lets loose a flurry of quick hard pecks,
But where he expected flesh
There's the glance, it seems, of one beak
Off another, the taste of metal instead of meat.

Ruffled now and out for blood, he hones in again
On the bird that stabs back at him.

ii.

Today, browsing, I come upon your likeness
In a woman on the web, her pretty breasts
And leanness and cascading black hair.

Without my glasses your face is there,
And your presence houseled again in the flesh,
And it is years again before your death.

iii.

The light papery comb of the wasp's nest
Tacked in a corner of the jamb, cloud-
Colored, capped like an acorn to its bough.
I watch as she fashions the airy apartments

As though gathering them from the air,
A first dusk filling the little cups
Beneath which she's suspended, tail up
And delicate, berthed already in her labors.

iv.

This evening, rain and some distant thunder,
Clouds towering to monument above the river.
The downpour drives me back indoors.
The unlit rooms, a cold sky in the mirrors.

v.

Across the road: bloodroot and twinleaf
And gill-over-the-ground,
Purple clematis sending out
Those vines for which there is no life

But entwining, a few wisps of last year's
Milkweed floating on the air . . .
At our wedding you were the *Primavera*,
A spray of baby's-breath at your ear,

The bouquet you tossed the bridesmaids.
There are still traces of fragrance
In the weave of that dress
I can't seem to part with, the cyme of its lace.

"The Clinging is empty in the middle,"
Says the *I Ching,* and cannot be filled.

CLEARING OUT THE CLOSET

i.

Undoing the top button, the blouse falls
From the hanger into my hands and there for a moment,
Before me, the wings of your collar-
Bones softly hover, and your naked, lovely throat.

ii.

The lavender sheen of lingerie, stockings
Like bundles of haze—all sachet-scented as that blouse,
And the pleated dress you wore that spring,
Full-blown as the irises at the side of the house.

FLORILEGIUM OF THE WILDFLOWERS IN NEW HOMESTEAD, PENNSYLVANIA

Loosestrife. Nightshade. Pearly everlasting.
A swatch of pye-weed like faded brocade . . .
You gathered them all and pressed them
Before pasting their cut-and-dried shapes.
All summer you'd kept it secret—
This present you were making of the hours
It took to fill the careful pages and notate them:
Flower, location, date. For you
Each green thing here was an article of faith,
Who thought of the days as a gift.

This morning I thought about it all again,
The first dayflowers blooming in the woods,
And the common morning glory.
In my bad time, in February,
I thought about arriving here, out of the hours
Of your dying and the huge drifting
Of houses away from the sun.
I ached to be transparent and beyond grief
As the shadows I watched fall, afternoons,
Through the boughs of the spruce.

Today, walking our familiar circuit of streets,
The flowers you found surround me,
As though turning a corner were turning a page.
Here, as there, I'm drawn to the pale ones
Which seem barely to fade—
The garden phlox and bindweeds,
Their yellow almost the ivory the sun gives

To lace. The evening primrose has it,
And the bracts of poor-man's peppergrass
That stumped you for days.

Those you didn't get to, you photographed.
Others, whose brief seasons stopped short,
You left pages for in back. Lady's-thumb
And trumpet vine. I'll set them for you
Here in these lines, press the loose spray
Of ironweed, the butter-and-eggs
I noticed growing at the foot of the road,
The way they almost bubble into sight,
Up from the gravel and broken ground
Which is the only given in their life.

BLUES PASSAGE

Stones in my passway, Robert Johnson sang—
Meaning, I think, the cursed ground east
Of Eden where he'd been cast—*and my road
seem dark as night.* I pile them behind me

In the garden aisles, little bits of rubble
The light has emptied from. For five summers
Now I've been freighting out clean fill
Seamed with ochre and shale-blue clay,

Hauling in soil and compost. All that time
I dreamt of loam as deep and rich as your body.
Back out this morning, after a day of rain,
I found the last bed covered with that dead

Mineral litter. *Hear me howlin' in my passway.*
So many stones, the hoe chinks going in.
They rise from inside the earth, you told me,
Laughing your great acceptance of things.

Later, all you asked for was a chance. *Please
don't block my road.* By then the only
Mercy was the coma. Again this morning,
When I went out, there were nothing but stones.

ELEGY ROSES

Our own life's a burial place . . .
　　—*Garry Wills on* The Man Who Shot Liberty
　　Valance

When, in that most tender of Ford's sorrows,
Tom sends Hallie the cactus rose,

The film—which is flashback and elegy
And halfway to its end—rests momentarily

In close-up of the paddle-shaped plant
Blossoming at evening above the sand.

Even there it looks like something meant for
The grave, makeshift and marker,

As if to point the way. Later, when Tom burns
Down the house he's been building for her,

The rooms flower with his grief,
The great dark billows of those flames.

Today in the garden, beside the bench I built
So you might rest your stricken bones,

I tamp the earth back about the roses
I've planted, already budding there—

Parade roses, cardinal red, which because hybrid
And domestic will need extra tending.

Something else to try to keep from dying,
Clustered and cut to size.

After the transplant, I remember writing
Now we begin the long hard work of recovery,

A kind of spring I believed in
As accompaniment to the year. It's spring again

And everything casts back your absence—
Cactus and petal, rose and stem and cell.

GARDEN DIPTYCH

1. *Garlic*

You planted it last year, late in the season
When the garden's small dynasties were at an end—

Grub-colored garlic, each clove a slivered moon
Slipped back into darkness—and no clue

In your blood work that you'd never see the green
Wands rising above their bed or the seed-casings

Forming like turbans. They even waived the biopsy.
This spring, to keep the plants from running to leaf,

I bent the stalks back toward the ground
Where the pale, segmented globes were rounding

Into the "stinking rose" of the herbals, the heal-all
That failed to, like everything else.

What's left except to braid the freshly dug bulbs
Into garlands, add your ashes to their bed?

2. *Groundhog*

Back here where you asked that your ashes be buried
Beneath the beams of cedar and rafters of fir,

It's slipped in again to plunder the entire crop
Of broccoli, leaving me with only the slavered stalks

And snapped-off leaves and sprung wires of the fence.
Next will be the Brussels sprouts and lettuce,

And the solace I've sought in growing things.
A crop of wrapped jade clouds, until this morning.

Beyond the stalks are the silktree and the bench I made
So you could sit in the feathery shade.

I'd banked the bed, hoed for grubs I might have missed.
My second summer without you, come to this.

And here I'd hoped to heal myself with the small,
Careful gestures I could fence off from failure and loss.

ORCHARDS

i.

Already, this morning,
The windfalls have been sorted,
The drops and lengths of firewood

Heaped beside the shed.
I move among them, sifting through
The seasons each has weathered,

Enjoying the whiff of resins,
The heft of the cord in my hands.
And then the axe-head,

Barking into timber,
Into oak stump and locust
As it slivers the resounding wood.

Beyond me, windrows fray
In showers of thin gold leaf.
The orchard deepens in the apple's core.

Logs chocked on the shed floor,
I work as though I meant it to last—
This wall I'll burn down all winter.

ii.

Buying winesaps, the hillside
Behind the stand streaming
With the bright crop

Burgeoning its boughs,
I think of how you ripened,
Carrying our sons,

The flower inside you
Swollen about its seeds,
Your breasts grown globed

And mortal as earthly fruit—
A woman become her own
Perfect miracle of blood

And loam and laughter,
Full moons, and the dark-
Leafed orchards of her hair.

iii.

A fleet seven of them float below me
In the creek: yellow
October apples, waxy suns,

Fat tallow glowing on the water
Like round brass lamps.
Each one is a lavish compacting

Of the flesh, bruised and translucent.
Each one dinted
In its hammered skin, washed golden

Among the shadows of the bridge
Where water's a wreckage
Of strewn cold fires.

iv.

We watched men in the trees
In February, dark hosts pruning
Among the sturdy limbs.

The green fire buckled
Beneath their feet. Their hands
Made motions, you told me,

As though braiding ribbons
Through their daughters' hair.
To me they resembled musicians

Who again that year were rehearsing
The grove's momentum into fruit.
I wanted you to see how,

Even in the tree limbs, the men
Had not left the earth in which
The staffs of their ladders took root.

v.

Dusk and cambium and smoke—
The hills grown transparent
As the glass door of the woodstove,

Sparrows flaying the chaff of light
Back into their branches.
Already this year the orchard aisles

Are empty, the apples you loved
Wizened black sacks.
Logs I stacked in September

Are still wet and tempered
With the last summer storms,
Flames climbing the kindling,

Our walls the color of late sun fallen
On the shafts of the trees: a red kiln
Glowing through heartwood.

Even the fox I saw last night
Was a long tray of embers
Flung teeming across the lawn.

THERE WERE FLOWERS ALSO IN HELL

i.

Crossing the bridge, alone in the falling snow,
I saw him below me clearing the pond for skaters.

He was running the small skiff of his shovel aground
In repeated strokes, upending its powdery cargoes,

A ghostly quadrant floating in the whiteness
Behind him where the light lay shelved as ice.

ii.

That first Lent after your passing, I spent hours
Sweeping up petals: limp, frost-stricken flames

Fallen in the aisles of the nursery where I worked.
Lilies for Easter, and those early flats of pansies

We'd take the row covers from in the mornings.
The petals would smear on the concrete floor.

BRAVING THE ELEMENTS

Lowe's Lawn and Garden Center, 2002

earth

Some days I'd wheel the clattering A-frame ladder
Into place against the building, lock it fast,
And spend hours stacking the great clay pots
On their shelves—two sets to the cubicle,
Rims clamped each about a circumference
Equal to their own. They'd take the full brunt
Of the weather, objects at rest until I hauled them
Back down, a wage-slave Atlas unshouldering
The globe. I passed whole weeks in a jumble,
Numb and newly widowed, with two sons at home.

fire

I'd thought at first to fit her ashes in a lidded jar,
Clay that had also passed through the flames
And been transfigured, changed back into earth,
But now all such matter seemed too inert.

water

Water-arum, trout-lily, salt-marsh aster were closer
To what I sought. Wild flowers the rains brought.
Days when stabs of gladness could make me weep.

air

In the crow's nest of the ladder I stood in a sky
The sparrows stormed, trapped inside the store.

SONNET

And once, in the wards of a big-box store,
I thought I saw you—a small, quick Eurydice
Disappearing among the aisles. Then once more
At the bar when friends turned their heads
And smiled and I could feel your quiet flesh
Breathing darkly behind me. Some nights,
Fixing supper, I think you must be caught in traffic
And keep looking up for headlights
Sweeping the bare woods at the end of our road.
Now no one's here to forgive me. No one
For me to accompany back into the world,
Those twelve clear months of remission
I watched you go from wheelchair to stroller
To evening walk, tarrying a little, on loan.

IRISH CATHOLIC

1. *Postcard*

A bad cold brought your Irish sojourn to a stop
That winter, halfway to Mayo
And the names in your address book.
A cold run of rainy days. In spite of its oils,
That thick wool sweater was sopping.
You brought a wrapped one back for me,
And a card from St. Kieran Street, Kilkenny:
ROBERTS' BOOKS. *Second hand*
& antiquarian books, maps & prints.
The name caught your eye, then mine
When you unpacked. Today I search through
The desk drawer for it, as if years later
I might find my way by retracing your steps,
As if they made such maps.

2. *Rosary*

So what were you like back then, decked out,
Making your first Communion,
Those colt's legs folded as you knelt?
Or before that, in the confessional?
When our sons came, you were adamant—
No baptisms or confirmations,
No days of fasting and abstinence—
Yet all your life you kept this brooch-shaped tin,
A stiletto-thin cross on its lid,
And inside: the cast-metal crucifix
And beaded string with which to reckon penance.

What had any of that to do with you,
Whose passion was keyed to storm clouds,
The plunging, wind-filled trees?

REMISSION

Not windsock nor kite nor traced shoal
    Of starlight, the goldfish still managed
        To take to the air above the pump-flushed

Waters of its tank and vanish completely
    From our sons' stunned room—a miracle
        Of absence we came to, that Christmas,

After the presents had been unwrapped.
    It was there this morning, the elder
        Informed us, nearly breathless with alarm.

His brother was sadder: *He was my favorite,*
    I gave him a name. Things die, we said,
        Moving the dresser away from the wall,

But where we thought to find the fish
    There was only baseboard, so we rifled
        The drawers as well, plunged deeper into

Mystery, and came up empty once more.
    It couldn't have just disappeared, I offered,
        My one article of faith. What's left except

To check back further beneath the dresser?
    And there it was, a little froth of the tropics
        Come to rest down in the dross

And wrappers, flat eye blankly staring,
    Colors fading already from the scales.
        What if we'd lost it for good there,

Seeping out oils, the oxygen thinned
        From its blood? What if I didn't discover
                That, scooped into the net, it twitched

And in the tank wobbled slowly toward
        The bottom, gills kneading, plumes
                Of dust fluttering all about it? How might

Any of us have guessed that by nightfall
        We'd find it, buoyant, flashing again
                Like tinsel in its billow of gauzy fins?

DRAWING HER BATH

Winter twilight: the sky a seam of mother-of-pearl
Reefed along the horizon,
Snow in the traceries of the trees.
Behind me the house fills with the quiet light
You loved to bathe in at the end of day.
I imagine you, passing before your mirror
Grown cloudy now with steam,
Then entering those scented waters, compassed
By comforting things—*stacked towels and bath salts,*
The honeycombed sponge—
The clear night mirrored in your eyes.
This is where memory keeps trying to fix the scene:
Not the bare limbs tatted by snowfall,
But the flush of your flesh through the steam.

MAGGIE GIBB
1958–2002

The thrum still fringing the loom
You'd thrum, each tamp of the batten.

Notes

"Days of Heaven": Hawkins recorded many versions of "Sweet Lorraine." The 1943 one, with his Swing Four, featured Eddie Heywood on piano.

"Pokeweed, Persimmons": Mu-ch'i was a thirteenth-century Japanese artist, whose painting *Persimmons* is alluded to; Edward Weston was a major twentieth-century American photographer whose peppers have become iconic.

"Morning Swim": Selkies, in Celtic mythology, are creatures that become human by shedding their skins; returning to the water, they become seals again.

"Blues Passage": Robert Johnson's "Stones in My Passway" can be found, most recently, on *The Centennial Collection,* from Columbia/Legacy.

"Elegy Roses": The poem incorporates details from John Ford's elegiac western.

"There Were Flowers Also in Hell": The title comes from William Carlos Williams's poem "Asphodel, That Greeny Flower."